Contents

D1349392

Introduction

In this book you will meet some children and adults who find learning things more difficult than most people.

They have a disability that affects how their brain works. There are several different disabilities of this kind.

▲ Some people have a disability that affects their movement as well as their learning.

▼ Contestants at the Special Olympics.

Everyone is different!

People are all different! For example, some of the people you will meet in this book are very good at sports. Some are not.

Most people with learning disabilities love to play and laugh, and enjoy being part of a family or a group of friends – though sometimes, when it's hard to learn, they can get frustrated or cross.

(Do you feel like that when you have trouble learning or understanding something, even though you are trying very hard?)

How do our brains work?

Even the most expert scientists understand only a little about how our brains work.

They do know that different parts of the brain are connected to our bodies, our senses, our feelings and our understanding.

But the brain is so complex, and in some ways so mysterious, that there are still many questions that cannot be answered. For example:

Why do you remember some things and forget others?

How do you know that some music sounds happy and some sounds sad?

Think for a moment. (What exactly IS thinking?) You can probably add many more questions of your own!

◀ Your eyes see these lines, and your brain makes sense of them.

It sifts through what it has learned about shapes like this and you know you see a box!

But which side of the box is nearest? Do you see it facing one way, then another? (See page 30.)

Everyday skills

People with learning disabilities may find it harder to develop everyday skills such as speaking clearly, or understanding and using money. They may have trouble concentrating, or reading instructions or filling in forms.

▶ Have you met someone who has a learning disability?

Think about learning

Think about the skills that people need to use in their everyday lives. The people on this page will give you some ideas.

How many of them are using numbers? How many are reading? Using numbers and reading are important basic skills.

What do you find helps you when you are learning a new skill?

Why do people memorise the Highway Code?

In their work, many people use the skills of gathering information, sifting out what is important and solving problems.

How many skills is this woman using at one time?

What basic skill must we have before we can learn to use money to buy things, and to save up for things we would like to buy in the future?

Do your grandparents find it harder than you do to set the video, or use a computer?

Why might people need to learn new skills as they grow older?

Do YOU have interests or hobbies where you must practise regularly to do them well?

Why might this time-table be hard to figure out?

Some things seem very hard to learn at first. But after we have done them many times, they become 'second nature': we find we can do them almost without thinking! Can you think of some examples?

BUS STOP

Learning disabilities

There are several types of learning disability. What causes them?

For some types of learning disability, we think we know the answer, or part of the answer, to this question. For other types, we don't.

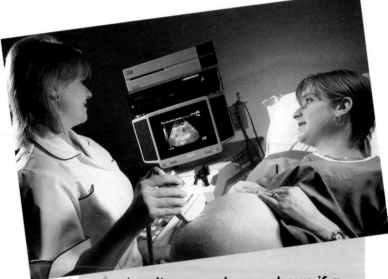

An ultra-sound scan shows if a mother's baby is growing well inside her. A picture of the baby is formed on the screen.

Down's syndrome

We all grow from tiny cells. One cell divides into two, two become four ... multiplying until a whole baby is made.

In each cell there are chromosomes, which carry information about how the cell works. Most people have 46 chromosomes in each cell. But some people have an extra chromosome number 21.

This extra chromosome affects how these people develop. For example, their eyes slant a little, and they do not usually grow as tall as their brothers and sisters. They also learn more slowly than others.

This is called Down's syndrome.

The younger boy has Down's syndrome.

Cerebral palsy

Cerebral palsy may affect a person's learning ability, movement, speech, sight and hearing. But it may affect only some of these.

Cerebral palsy is caused by injury to a baby's brain. The injury may happen while the baby is inside the mother, or when the baby is being born, or later, if a young baby becomes very ill.

Each person with cerebral palsy has different abilities and disabilities. It depends which parts of the brain are injured, and how badly.

Autism

Some people have a particular problem responding to other people. They have trouble understanding expressions on people's faces, and in communicating.

It seems that their brains do not sift or balance information as most people's brains do. They may take an interest in just one surprising subject like weather forecasts, or burglar alarms, and take little interest in anything else.

This type of disability is called autism.

Special exercises

Some babies who have cerebral palsy can be helped by gentle exercises of their arms, legs and neck.

The exercises encourage healthy parts of the brain to take over some of the work that would have been done by parts that are injured.

In the film *Rainman*, Dustin Hoffman plays the part of a man with autism. The man has a brilliant memory for numbers.

Mystery talent

Some people with autism have one particular talent (for example, in mental arithmetic or art), even though they have difficulty with everyday skills. It is a mystery why this happens.

Meet some people with learning disabilities

Anna Frizell-Armitage

Here's Anna at a tennis lesson, and with her friends in year 5 of Merryhills Primary School.

Anna has Down's syndrome, and needs extra support in some lessons. As well as the teacher, there is another grown-up, called a classroom assistant, to help.

Anna loves singing – especially the songs from *The Sound of Music* and *Mary Poppins*. She is good at remembering the words.

Anna sings in the choir after school on Wednesdays. She also goes to Chicken Shed – a theatre company that encourages children to take part in shows and plays, whether they have disabilities or not.

Anna has two younger sisters, Amelia and Esther. They don't have Down's syndrome.

On holiday, Anna and her sisters saw an owl, and Anna wrote a poem about it.

My brother

I'm David Grossmith and this is me (on the left) with my brother Simon. He is 5, and he has autism.

It's hard to explain what that means. He's got learning difficulties. His concentration doesn't last very long.

He does some funny things – like once he painted himself with spots. He said he had chicken pox.

At play group, he couldn't join in the games, and spent a lot of time under the table.

He often repeats what you just said, or he says something from the TV over and over again.

Simon used to hurt me quite a lot. He seemed horrible, I suppose. It's better since he went to school. He plays with me more. Sometimes I show him how to do things. He loves playing on the computer.

He doesn't get invited to parties much, because of how he behaves. I don't like it if he is called silly. He's not silly. He can't help it. I think he's quite a nice boy. I like my brother.

Simon's cat Nutty won top prize in a national competition. It was because Nutty has never scratched or hurt Simon.

Meet Charlotte Ah-hing

Charlotte is playing in her garden with her big sister Lucy, and friends Gavin and Wayne.

Charlotte is 8 years old. Because she has a severe form of cerebral palsy she cannot stand without support.

Also, her brain does not control her swallowing muscles very well. She can easily choke. This is why she has to be given liquid food through a tube straight into her stomach.

Charlotte cannot talk, but she can see and hear. She communicates in her own way with facial expressions and sounds.

What really makes her laugh is going over bumps in the car!

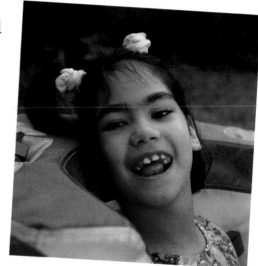

Charlotte goes to a special school for disabled children. One day her class went on a field trip by the river. They felt the leaves and smelled the flowers.

Charlotte loves to listen to music. She also likes the sound of dolphins, and the sound of the sea. In her school concert she played the maraccas and the drum.

Jehan Morris

I'm Jehan and I am 16 years old. My springer spaniel, Max, is just one and very lively!

I would like to work with animals when I leave school.

I go to school in Tottenham, but I support Arsenal. My brother supports Manchester United and my dad supports Spurs!

This year I went to Dominica in the Caribbean with my mum and my sister Pia. It is where my mum was born. The three of us go to church together too. Pia and I are in the Girls' Brigade.

Jehan's mother explains that Jehan has a very rare condition. Since she was born, a slow-growing tumour squeezed her brain, affecting how it worked.

Brothers and sisters

Probably all brothers and sisters sometimes get on well and sometimes don't!

The brothers and sisters of the people in this chapter are great friends to them. They stick up for them and help in practical ways.

Many children with a disabled brother or sister show special kindness.

But it's natural sometimes to feel cross or left out if parents have to give more time to the disabled child than to others, or if the family has to be organized around the disabled child's needs.

Dyslexia

Some people have a long-term difficulty with reading, writing and spelling. This is called dyslexia.

Think about the box on page 7. Did it seem to face first one way, then another? Your brain had to interpret what your eyes saw. This may give you an idea of what dyslexia is like.

About half the people with dyslexia have trouble with numbers as well as words.

In Britain, at least 2 people in every 100 have dyslexia.

You can be very intelligent (clever) and dyslexic.

Dyslexia was officially recognized only in 1975.

Talking about dyslexia

People with dyslexia describe writing:

'I can't remember the order of the letters or which way round they go.'

'I used to write backwards, like in a mirror.'

'My hands don't do what my brain tells them to.'

People with dyslexia describe reading:

'It's like the TV aerial not catching the signal, so the picture is fuzzy.'

'Sometimes the words seem to move around on the page.'

'I have to concentrate so hard on each word, to figure out what it is, that I lose the meaning of the sentence.'

A court case

In 1997 Pamela Phelps won a court case in Britain about her dyslexia.

Pamela said that she had suffered unhappiness and loss of confidence because her school had not recognized her learning difficulty. The judge said that Pamela should be given compensation (money) to make up for what she had suffered.

▲ Pamela Phelps (right) with her lawyer.

Things that help

If you are dyslexic, it is easy to lose confidence. You have to keep trying very hard to do what seems easy to other people.

Reading aloud is a worry. What if you say a wrong word and it sounds foolish? The worst problem is other people not understanding the difficulty you have.

But there are practical things that help. Reading is easier when there is lots of space between the lines of print, and between paragraphs.

Coloured type, or a tinted page, are sometimes better than black on white.

Using a word processor makes your work neat and your letters the right way round. You can also use spell-check.

▶ Film star Whoopi Goldberg is one of many famous people who have dyslexia. Others include: rower Steve Redgrave (four times Olympic gold medallist), politician Michael Heseltine, and actors Susan Hampshire and Tom Cruise.

Working together

There are around one million people in Britain who have some form of learning disability.

The largest organization for them and their families is called MENCAP.

A MENCAP poster. ▶

MENCAP

MENCAP works to find out what people with learning disabilities need, and puts them in touch with others who can help.

mencap
making the most of life

Local projects
In many towns and cities, local projects support people who have learning disabilities.

For example, in London, the Paddington Integration Project (PIP) helps young adults develop the skills they need to get about in the city.

Working Support, in Wapping, helps people find a job. Then it offers help and advice to these people in their first few weeks at work.

MENCAP provides homes, clubs, colleges and holidays. It also provides help in finding jobs.

MENCAP was founded in 1946 by Judy Fryd, a parent. At that time there was no organization to advise and support the families of children with learning disabilities.

Today MENCAP has over 500 local groups, 4,000 staff and 50,000 members.

Botton Village

Botton Village is in the North Yorkshire Moors. More than 300 people live there. Around half of them have learning disabilities. They come from far and wide, to live together in the village's lovely old farm houses.

Tea break at High Farm, Botton. ▷

Each person in the village has a job to suit his or her skills. There are five farms, a bakery, a wood workshop, a printing press, a food centre and a church.

Botton villagers make wooden toys and woven scarves, jam, bread, and many other things. These are sold to visitors at the two village shops.

There are 30 similar villages in Britain, Europe and Africa. They are called Camphill communities.

In each community, people are valued for what they can do. They have a secure home, useful work, and lots of friends and activities.

▼ **Botton farm workers.**

◁ **The wood workshop.**

At home

Some grown-ups with learning disabilities live at home with their parents. Others are able to live on their own.

Those who need support outside their families usually live in small groups, in homes where staff can help them.

▲ This young man lives at home with his parents.

▼ Philip Cole taught himself to play the guitar. He loves to put on shows for his friends.

A home for twelve

Philip Cole lives in a home that provides care in the community. Twelve people with learning disabilities live in the home. The three or four staff make sure that things run smoothly.

Philip has his own room with a shower and a toilet. Everyone shares the kitchen, dining and lounge areas, and the garden.

Everyone takes turns to cook and wash up. Philip's favourite thing to cook is curry. He puts in lots of chillies to make it taste strong. His friends say it is sometimes too strong! But they all like the fresh fruit salad Philip makes.

The Hunter family

Jane and Andrew Hunter live in London. They have their own house and garden.

When their son Thomas was born, some people wondered how well Andrew and Jane would be able to look after him. Andrew has learning difficulties and Jane has Down's syndrome. But Thomas has no disabilities.

At first, Jane was given help from support workers to care for Thomas.

'We don't have support now. People think we can't cope, but we do,' Jane explains.

▲ Jane, Andrew and Thomas outside their house.

At present, Andrew stays at home to help look after Thomas.

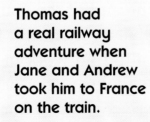

◄ Thomas had a real railway adventure when Jane and Andrew took him to France on the train.

Before, Andrew worked as a gardener and in a warehouse. He says he worries about the household bills, but he works everything out carefully and they manage.

Jane passed her GCSE English Literature exam at school, and she loves books. She enjoys reading to Thomas. Of course, his favourites are the stories of Thomas the Tank Engine!

Developing skills

Some children who have learning disabilities go to special schools (for children with disabilities). Some go to mainstream (ordinary) schools.

▲ **Adults with learning disabilities at a painting class.**

But learning does not end with school. The adults in the pictures here are continuing their learning in various ways.

Mainstream schools

In Britain, more mainstream schools than ever before include children with disabilities.

Each child is considered individually. If he or she needs extra support to understand the lessons, then this support is given.

Training to be cooks

The picture on the right shows some students at a further education college. They are on a catering course.

At the end of the course they will receive a certificate. This will help them to find work in a restaurant or school canteen, or anywhere where cooking is done.

Re-learning

This man became disabled when his head was injured in an accident. He finds it hard to do things he did before. Using the computer at the hospital is helping to improve his concentration, memory and movement.

A trainee gardener

The young woman above is training as a gardener. Afterwards, she may use her skills to work in a park or a college, or anywhere where there are flowers and shrubs and trees and lawns to care for.

People First

Adults with learning disabilities want to do things for themselves. They do not want other people to decide everything for them.

An organization called People First offers training in self-advocacy – which means speaking up for yourself.

People First encourages people with disabilities to put across their point of view about their abilities, needs and rights.

Going to work

Going out to work means using lots of skills. Count all the skills the people here are using, at work and out and about.

People with disabilities have the same right as everyone else to show what they can do. This is called Equal Opportunities.

'I meet lots of different people in my job. I have to get their orders right, and be helpful and friendly.'

'Acting in the Drama Festival means remembering my part as well as working in a team.'

'Sometimes I go on a training course to bring my skills up to date.'

THE CRAFT ST

DRAMA FESTIVAL

THEATRE

TICKETS

e Café Pierre

MENU

'I enjoy talking to people.'

'There is a lot to learn, but the manager is always there to give me advice. I have learned to listen carefully.'

'I made an Action Plan. I decided what type of job I wanted. Then I planned the steps needed to achieve it.'

'At the Job Club we learn how and where to look for jobs. We practise how to fill in an application form and how to present ourselves well in an interview.'

'I enjoy working with animals. It gives me responsibility and confidence in myself.'

'Following the rules about health and safety is an important part of my job.'

Going to work means getting there on time each day.

It means wearing the right clothes.

It means communicating with other people.

It means following instructions and doing your best.

'I like pay-day. Earning money makes me independent, and I love to plan what to spend it on!'

Leisure time

People keep very busy in their leisure time!

▶ Andrew Hunter (*see page 21*) loves drawing and painting. This picture was created by him.

◀ Rehearsing for a play.

Gateway Clubs

Sixty thousand people with learning disabilities belong to MENCAP's national network of Gateway Clubs.

The clubs organize many exciting activities and holidays for members of all ages. Non-disabled friends are welcome too.

▲ Learning to canoe on an activity holiday.

MORNINGS
6.30 Get up.
8.00-9.30 Go to work as a cleaner at a local store.

AFTERNOONS
Monday: Aqua aerobics
Tuesday: Swimming
Wednesday: Keep-fit and dance
Thursday: Art and cooking (college)
Friday: Computer class

EVENINGS
Social club.

A busy life!

Susan Millard lives with three friends in a MENCAP flat. She leads a busy life.

The social clubs she goes to sometimes meet at a pub and play darts or snooker. Sometimes they play badminton.

At home, Susan likes to listen to tapes – very loud, say her flat-mates!

Sports champion

Joanne Newman is a gold medal winner in swimming. She won her award at the National Championships of the Special Olympics. Here's Joanne competing in the long-jump, another of her events.

Glossary

aqua aerobics
exercise done in the swimming pool.

autism
a condition that affects a person's social and communication skills.

Camphill movement
network of working communities inspired by Christian ideas, where people with learning disabilities play their full part in a shared way of life.

care in the community
the system of providing care and support for people with disabilities in family-sized homes – rather than the big hospital-like institutions of years ago.

cerebral palsy
'Cerebral' means to do with the brain; 'palsy' means paralysed, or not working properly. Cerebral palsy can affect a person's movement or speech, without affecting his or her learning ability.

Down's syndrome
a condition caused by human cells having 47 chromosomes instead of the usual 46 (made up of 23 pairs). Each cell has an extra chromosome number 21. The condition is named after the doctor who first studied it.

dyslexia
difficulty with words. ('Dys' means 'difficulty' and 'lexia' means 'words' in Greek.) Dyslexic people may improve their reading, writing and spelling skills as they grow older, but they do not completely overcome the problem.

Gateway Clubs
network of activity clubs for people with learning disabilities, organized by MENCAP.

GCSE
General Certificate of Secondary Education. Exams usually taken in secondary school.

MENCAP
national organization for people with learning disabilities and their families.

ultra-sound scan
a technique used in hospitals to see inside a person's body. Sound waves are directed at a part of the body. The waves bounce back to make a picture on a screen of what they have found.

Useful addresses

MENCAP National Centre,
123 Golden Lane,
London EC1Y 0RT
Tel 0171 454 0454
(includes book shop and
information service)
For local groups of
MENCAP, see your
telephone directory.

National Autistic Society,
393 City Road,
London EC1V 1NE
tel 0171 833 2299

Botton Village,
Danby,
Whitby,
Yorkshire YO21 2NJ
tel 01287 660871
(a member of the
Association of Camphill
Communities)

The Brainwave Centre,
Centre for Rehabilitation
and Development from
Brain Injury,
Huntworth Gate,
Bridgwater,
Somerset TA6 6LQ
tel 01278 429089

**British Dyslexia
Association**,
98 London Road,
Reading,
Berks RG1 5AU
tel 01734 668271

**Centre for Studies on
Inclusive Education**,
1 Redland Close,
Elm Lane, Redland,
Bristol BS6 6UE
tel 0117 923 8450

**Chicken Shed Theatre
Company**,
Chase Side,
Southgate,
London N14 4PE
tel 0181 449 7744

**Down's Syndrome
Association**,
155 Mitcham Road,
London SW17 9PG
tel 0181 682 4001

**Paddington Integration
Project (PIP)**,
404 Edgware Road,
London W2 6NE
tel 0171 258 1122

People First,
Instruments House,
207-215 King's Cross Road,
London WC1X 9DB
tel 0171 713 6400

SCOPE (for people with
cerebral palsy)
Head Office,
12 Park Crescent,
London W1N 4EQ
tel 0171 636 5020
For regional offices and
local shops, see your
telephone directory.

Skill,
National Bureau for
Students with Disabilities,
336 Brixton Road,
London SW9 7AA
tel 0171 274 0565
information service:
0171 978 9890

IN AUSTRALIA

Autistic Association of NSW,
41 Cook Street,
Forestville NSW 2087
tel 02 9452 5088

Index

When you looked at the box picture on page 7, you may have seen the box facing this way

and then this way

Did you keep seeing the box first one way, then the other, so that it seemed to jump about on the page?

The lines that make up the picture on page 7 confuse your brain. It recognizes the front of the box in one position and then in another.

The picture is an optical illusion.